I0508828

All my...

notebooks

Author represented by Tibor Kleinberg

Vali-g@gmx.at

ISBN: 9781712816509

Hello there, i am your notebook!

You might wonder why you are reading this right now.

You know, i am as alive as you are! In fact, i im kind of a reflection of you.

Also, i am very curious and i really want to get to know you and i definetly want to know what keeps you busy all day long!

No worries! I can keep secrets for myself ;-)

You chose me so that you can put everything down on paper and i chose you because you are great!

Great and interesting and you got a lot of other qualities

i would like to discover while you are writing into me.

With that being said, have fun and PLEASE don't put me aside. Keep writing! ☺

xoxo your notebook

www.ingramcontent.com/pod-product-compliance
Lightning Source LLC
Chambersburg PA
CBHW030706220526
45463CB00005B/1928
9781712816509